TAZIE EFFECT

Turning Life's Defining Moments Into Personal and Professional Greatness

Heather Whittaker

Heather Whittaker

Pen-Tech Professional

The Tazie Effect
by Heather Whittaker

ISBN: 978-0-9820962-0-8
Library of Congress Control Number: 2008936899

Pen-Tech Professional
PO Box 7123
Appleton, WI 54912
www.thetazieeffect.com

Copy Editing/Proofreading: Cheryl Pinno
Cover Design & Illustrations: Rohde Marketing & Design Group Inc.
Page Layout/Design: Shawn Morningstar

Special Thanks

To Mary—Thank you for all of your love and support through the writing process. If it weren't for you, Taz's story would never have been told.

About the Author

Ms. Whittaker has a Masters degree in Organizational Leadership, 15 years management experience, and is an adjunct faculty member for Cardinal Stritch University's College of Business. She lives in Rural Wisconsin with her partner, Mary, and their 2 Miniature Pinschers, Taz and Tinker. For more information regarding Tazieroo or to order additional copies of "The Tazie Effect", please visit www.thetazieeffect.com.

Table of Contents

Preface

As a manager of people, my career has been filled with what I call "learning opportunities." Opportunities presented to me by my direct and indirect reports that offered a chance to better myself as a manager. Everyday I was faced with questions and decisions that needed to be made; all of which were defining moments for my career. When I made an effective decision, I walked away a stronger person and better manager. When I made an ineffective decision, I inevitably would be presented that "learning opportunity" again in the future. My mistakes became some of the greatest "learning opportunities" I could imagine.

As a leader, learning opportunities are not necessarily mistakes. In fact, whether an experience is from a positive or negative situation, it results in growth to all those involved. As people grow in their careers aspiring to climb the proverbial corporate ladder, those defining moments or learning opportunities never disappear. The interactions continue presenting themselves for managers to grow, learn, and develop into stronger leaders. This is one of the reasons I enjoy leading people. There is so much to learn from other people and being in a leadership position provides a front row seat.

What happens, however, when managers get burned out? What happens when leaders are de-motivated and stop learning? What happens when individuals become more inclined to take the easy road?

When managing people, there are constant challenges to overcome. Attitude problems, attendance issues, back logs of volumes, missed objectives, outlandish bonus expectations, staffing shortages, technological challenges and any number of other unpredictable issues take their toll on a manager. Over many years, these challenges can result in an ever growing level of pessimism making it hard to motivate and drive the team. Employees will in turn begin to see the decline in management's dedication to the team, as well as the company vision. Thus, a downward spiral begins which is difficult to turn around in the absence of strong leadership.

So, who motivates the motivator? Who leads the leader? How do people find the original drive and determination that first pointed them in the direction of not just management, but also becoming effective leaders?

This book presents ten principles of leadership for new managers to help them find and keep that very drive and determination when faced with on-going challenges. They are key principles that result in successful leadership and will help managers maintain their focus and motivation.

Ten lessons in leadership learned from my 6 lb. dog.

Yes, that's right. I said dog. Allow me to introduce you to Taz. A 6-lb, black and tan Miniature Pinscher also affectionately known as Tazie Roo, Baby Woo, Sweet Pea, Pumpkin, My Little Black Jelly Bean, and Tazie Rooper. She is a bundle of energy, and over the course of the last 12 years, she has experienced more challenges than some people will experience over a 40 year career. She has, however, conquered each of those challenges successfully resulting in a great amount of happiness within our household.

Now, I'm sure you're thinking there is no way you can learn anything about leadership from Taz. Some of you are probably even questioning why you bought this book. I encourage you to read on, however. As I worked through a slump in my own career, it was only then that I realized each of the principles which pushed me to be a leader in the first place are exemplified in how Taz lives her life.

She is 12 years old, 6-lbs strong and still looks like a puppy resulting in her being loved by everyone who meets her. Through everything that has happened to her, she continues to grow and accomplish great things. It's the Tazie Effect. As leaders we can only hope to be as accomplished in our careers as Taz has been through her life. As a new leader, take these principles as you move forward and build your skills. They will serve you well.

Chapter 1

Be An Optimist

"We are what we think. All that we are arises with our thoughts. With our thoughts, we make the world."

—Buddha

Taz was born the runt of the litter. She was small and appeared to be undernourished; however, she was by far the cutest of all her siblings. Although a small dog, she had huge feet and big floppy ears, so we believed she would grow to be a larger miniature pinscher in the 11–18 lb range. What we did not realize at the time was Taz had physical challenges that would prevent her growth.

Taz had Legg-Calve-Perthe's syndrome which we were told meant that she had a problem with her rear legs and hip joints. One of them was set to never develop properly which could eventually result in paralysis. Fortunately, the problem was caught early on when we noticed it was becoming difficult for Taz to get around. To correct the problem, we worked with a naturalist who started Taz on a vitamin program. In addition, we worked with a local therapist who utilized the Feldenkreis technique to stimulate her muscles and the blood flow through her legs. After several months of work, Taz's legs started to improve. She started building strength in her hind legs, but that was only the beginning.

Taz also began having problems with her joints resulting in her kneecaps dislocating. A condition called Patellar Luxation. We would literally have to pop them back into place which was an extremely painful process…for all of us.

This led to surgery where the veterinarian put pins in both rear knees and after Taz recovered, we did additional therapy involving swimming.

The lesson learned...through all of the trauma, this little 6-lb bundle of energy never gave up. She wanted in the worst way to run with her sisters. (We also had two other dogs at the time.) And, run is what she was bound and determined to do. For any of you who have suffered from joint pain, broken bones or any similar challenge, you can imagine the amount of pain this little girl faced everyday. Regardless, she never exhibited any signs of depression. She never cried. She never refused to swim. Instead, her full focus was on being able to run. She was an optimist.

OPTIMISM—THE SECRET TO SUCCESS

As a leader, there will be times when you find the company vision to be a challenge or you are faced with stressful projects and impossible deadlines. There may be directives issued by higher ups which you find easy to pick apart. Whatever the situation, it's important to remember it is easy to be a pessimist. To be an effective leader, however, optimism is the requirement. Messages of doom and gloom will spread through your team like a wild fire. Cynicism and doubt have no place in business.

Conversely, messages of optimism, success, and achievement will resonate through your team as well. People inherently want to be on the winning team. If the message they receive from their leader is one of optimism and impending success, they will strive to achieve those goals. Set clear and challenging expectations. Focus on the positive. As the leader, you set the tone for your team. If you fail to publicly identify why a plan, change, or challenge will not work, chances are your team will also fail to identify the signs.

If you publicly and optimistically support a plan, change, or challenge; your team will also reflect your optimism.

"WILL I HAVE A JOB?"

One prime example of a situation requiring optimism is any type of merger, acquisition, or consolidation a company faces. Successful navigation of a project of this magnitude can involve facilitating best practice sessions, reviewing current strategies and possibly changing direction, consolidating work, and upgrading systems. All of those initiatives can result in a reduced workforce and you may in fact manage yourself out of a job.

Regardless, the company expects you to support the initiative no matter what the end result. They also expect you to publicly support the initiative in front of your team ensuring a continual drive for productivity and employee engagement during a stressful time of change.

When I worked for a local bank, we transitioned through that very scenario consolidating processes due to a merger. The first question that popped into my head as well as the heads of my staff was "Will I have a job?" We were taking on the name of the other organization and all of our processes were duplicated in their Minneapolis, MN office.

We moved through the projects associated with the merger making decisions based on what was best for the bank as a whole, and in the end, processes actually moved from the Minnesota location to our Wisconsin location. Our positive attitudes, commitment to doing what was best for the bank as a whole, and our overall support of the initiative ultimately moved the work our way. (Keep in mind the work easily could have shifted to Minnesota.) We considered ourselves lucky, but professionalism played a part as well.

LESSON LEARNED

What's best for your organization is not necessarily what's best for you as an individual. As a leader the company expects you to understand that and also expects you to do what's best. If it results in new work, there's a new challenge for you to face. If it results in you losing your job, there's also a new challenge for you to face. Moving on with optimism is the only option.

For Taz, moving on and conquering the next challenge was her only option. She maintained a positive attitude and was successful as a result of that attitude. As a leader, make your attitude positive regardless of the situation and your team is sure to follow.

Chapter 2

Put People First

"To get the full value of joy, you must have people to divide it with."

—Mark Twain

Most dogs get excited when you arrive home from work, someone new arrives at the house for a visit or a delivery driver arrives with a package. Some pee on the floor because they can't control their excitement. Some instinctively want to protect their owner and attack the visitor. Someone new at the door can be either a positive or negative experience.

For little Tazie Rooper, it doesn't matter who you are or why you are visiting, it is ALWAYS a welcome surprise. She starts with a high pitched, shrill bark which is enough to send you searching for ear plugs. When the door finally opens, her little half inch long stub of a tail wiggles so fast you would think it was going to fall off. She then begins a combination of jumping and spinning while continuing to bark. Combine that with her floppy ears and it doesn't matter who you are, you are compelled to either bend down and start petting her or grab her mid—jump to cuddle. If you choose to bend down and pet her, beware...she will jump up on your arm before you know what happened, and you will find yourself dropping whatever package, purse, or bag you were holding. There is just no two ways about it. Taz LOVES people. And as a result, people LOVE Taz. I have witnessed her win over the hearts of even the most determined of dog haters.

JUMPING AND SPINNING

Now, as a professional, I do not suggest that when someone comes to your office, you greet them by jumping and spinning.

I do, however, suggest...

- Smile and show enthusiasm when in the presence of your team.
- Get to know your employees along with the issues that impact them and the things that inspire them.
- Ask for and provide feedback from all levels of your organization several times a year. Employee's opinions are important as is your opinion of the employee. Open, honest, two-way communication goes a long way.
- Make time to listen whenever an employee needs the time.
- Celebrate your employee's successes and recognize the importance of their contributions.
- Say "Thank You"...a lot!

Just as a chain is only as strong as its weakest link, leaders are only as great as their team. Managers are judged by their team's productivity, quality, sales, and overall performance. Leaders, on the other hand, are judged by all the same criteria with one exception. They are also judged by their effectiveness to inspire and motivate their people. It's important to recognize as the leader that you are not just the manager of the process but also the cheerleader of the people.

THE FIRST 30 DAYS

During your first 30 days leading a new team, take the time to meet individually with every employee. Tell them your expectations. Your new to the group and do not necessarily have the same expectations as the previous manager. Your employees deserve to hear your expectations up front vs. finding out through trial and error. Ask for their expectations as well. Employees have expectations of their leaders and they vary from person to person. You will be one step closer to earning your employees respect if you not only ask, but allow time for each employee to share their individual expectations with you.

Learn about their personal lives. Find out what impacts them and what is most important to them during the course of a day. Give them a chance to ask you questions. Find shared experiences. Maybe you both love Italian food. Maybe you've both taken vacations to Europe. Finding the little things you have in common helps build a bond from the start, and showing an interest in your employee demonstrates your dedication to not just the team but the individual.

KNOW WHAT'S IMPORTANT

One of the best ways to put your people first is to know what's important to each individual. Before leaving for the day on Friday, ask what your employees have planned for the weekend. On Monday morning, ask how they enjoyed their event. For example, one employee may be having a birthday party for their child. Nothing shows you care more than asking about the party on Monday morning. It means the world to an employee when their leader remembers little details. (If remembering is a struggle for you, write them down and leave yourself a note. Monday morning, it will be the first thing you see reminding you to go out, walk the floor and say good morning.)

For some employees, their children or spouse may be what's most important. Keep in mind, however, that not all employees have children or a spouse. Some employees may have season tickets for the local baseball team, so time off may be what's of most importance. Letting them go home an hour early on game day tells them you care.

MAKE A CONNECTION

One of the first managers I ever had was especially skilled at making everyone feel connected to the team. In my cubicle, I had no personal items, no decorations. On one particular day, my manager sat down on my desk and emphatically proclaimed, "Heather, you need a picture." She proceeded to draw a stick dog on a piece of copy paper and pinned it on my wall.

"There, that looks better. Next week I'll draw you a brother or sister." She then walked away leaving me and my neighbors laughing.

She continued to check back once a week asking if I had any new pictures or did I want her to draw another. She was just quirky, but that quirkiness connected me to the team. Eventually, I brought in a personal picture which lead to a personal connection with my peers and I felt connected to the team.

Taz makes every visitor to our house feel special because she puts them first. You can encourage top performance in your team if you also put your people first. Be glad they are part of your team and express your appreciation. If you LOVE your team, your team will LOVE you.

Ok, and, an occasional "jump and spin" might not hurt. Employees like to see their boss act weird once in a while. (Just make sure it's "once in a while".)

Chapter 3

Be The Boss

"To be able to lead others, a man must be willing to go forward alone."

— **Harry S Truman**

Our little Baby Woo is definitely little, but shhhh, don't tell her. She is 110% big dog spirit trapped in a little dog body. She shows no fear regardless of the circumstance and is always trying to be the lead dog. Taz is the baby in our family, but she'll have none of that. She and her sister, Tinker, have gotten in no less than 15 fights over the course of her life all of which had a poor outcome for Taz. Tinker is the alpha dog, has a personality I can only describe as misunderstood, and she has no patience for Taz's puppy games. Believe it or not, Tinker shows great restraint when attacking Taz, but Baby Woo keeps coming back for more. She truly shows no fear and believes of every fight that this is the one where she will prevail.

She's not even afraid of a Great Dane more than 20 times her own weight. When Taz was 6 years old, we took her with us to the local Humane Society pet walk. We had volunteered to help with the event and were scheduled to assist with registration. What kind of trouble could Taz get into sitting on our laps at a registration table? She was out of her element, so she was behaving very well. Taz has always liked to watch things, so she was sitting innocently on my lap looking around just watching all the people. There was no spinning or jumping, no excitement, no barking. She was quiet and did I mention sitting on my lap.

A walker approached our table with her equally well behaved Great Dane. He walked up close to the front of the table and rested his nose on the edge. He was an absolutely beautiful animal. As we took the pledge sheet from the Great Dane's owner, Taz lunged across the table snapping at the Great Dane attempting to take a chunk out of his nose. No warning, no provocation. She simply was not going to tolerate this big dog standing at her table. Needless to say…PEOPLE love Taz, other dogs, not so much. She is very much the boss in her world and makes sure other dogs know it.

CREATE SOME DISTANCE

As leaders who manage people, it is important to remember you are also the boss in your world and it is equally important that you keep that distinction. Leaders need to put their people first and take a personal interest in employee's lives; however, this needs to be done without getting too personal or friendly. Developing close, personal friendships outside work with employees directly reporting to you will only lead to perceptions of favoritism when at work. It also creates an uncomfortable situation for you and the employee if ever there's a performance issue that needs to be addressed. Your "friend" expects you to be lenient; however, you go out of your way to prove there is no favoritism resulting in hurt feelings.

When promoted to a Team Lead, Supervisor, or Manager position, there's a chance some individuals who were your friends yesterday are now your team members today and that can be a difficult adjustment. Do yourself a favor and establish boundaries from the start. Friday night dinners are not a good idea if they involve direct reports. The Saturday bowling league should probably now be off limits. Invited to your friends wedding? It's OK to attend the ceremony, but you should probably steer clear of the reception. Social engagements that have a tendency to get out of control can result in stories Monday morning that affect your credibility as the leader or even worse, can result in the loss of your job.

I know of one particular manager who actually did lose his job because of this type of situation. What started out as a leisurely boat trip for a group of employees, transitioned to a few drinks at a local tavern and a friendly game of pool. From there, one of the employees was in no condition to drive, so the manager took him home. One thing lead to another and the next thing we heard was that a fist fight broke out between the employee and the manager. The police were involved and it wasn't a good situation for either individual. End result—the manager lost his job.

Your relationships need to change to ensure your success as the leader.

THE COMPANY COMES FIRST

In my first ever leadership role, I was a dispatcher responsible for 20+ drivers. It was typical for the drivers and me to go out for drinks after work or to some other event during the week. Some were on a dart league. Others were in a bowling league and these people were my new group of friends. After a few months in my new position, there was a morning when I then needed to make a decision whether I was their friend or their dispatcher.

Several of us had been out the previous evening and did not get in until very early the next morning. Two of my drivers were in no condition to drive and as their boss, I needed to report that situation to the garage manager. Were my "friends" upset with me? You bet. Was the manager disappointed?

Of course. Did I do the right thing? Absolutely. I needed to step up and recognize the distinction that as of 6:00 am, I was now their boss. They then taught me that as of 5:00 pm, I was still their boss. Let's just say I was never invited to join the dart league.

ONLY "FRIENDS" WELCOME

At another point in my career with a different employer, I was invited to a Halloween party at the home of one of my employees. I was new to the company, liked this individual and thought it would be a good way to show my staff I was human too. After all, it was Halloween which by its very definition is fun. While at the party, my partner and I just sat and watched everyone. My employee's family members were cordial and we had a few short conversations, but they really didn't have anything to say to the boss. The employees who were present, said "Hi" to me but didn't really know what else to say since their only interaction with me was from work. After an acceptable amount of time, we exited leaving them to their fun. On Monday morning, all I heard was how great this party was. Everyone told me I should have stuck around because of all the antics. I apparently missed a great party. Personally, I believe it was because I left that they had such a great time. What I realize now is as their boss, I did not belong at the party.

BE CAREFUL OF THE DOG SITTER

The importance of getting to know your employees should not be overlooked. It's important to remember, however, that personal relationships should be avoided. There's a fine line of which every leader should be cognizant.

My partner had one employee who shared a passion for dogs and over the course of time, we had asked her to do some dog sitting. We eventually became close friends and did a lot together outside work. That friendship ended, however, when she stole some money from us. Being our dog sitter, we had given her a key to our house and she used that key to take advantage.

Our friendship was over. Our trust of others diminished. And worst of all, she made the issue public at work creating a very uncomfortable situation for the managers and others in the department as well.

LESSON LEARNED

Highly effective leaders are friendly with staff members, show them respect, have fun when appropriate, treat their employees fairly, and do it all because THEY ARE THE BOSS. Remember, leaders are also managers just as responsible for the process as the people. Be the boss in your world.

Chapter 4

Training, Training, and More Training

"Enlarge the opportunity and the person will expand to fill it."

— Eli Ginzberg

For anyone who has owned a dog, you are all too familiar with the need for training. They need to learn from early on that you are the boss. They also need to be socialized so they can be around other dogs and need to know how to behave around people. They need to learn their boundaries in the house and yard, and let us not forget the need to be house broken.

Well, if you have had experience with Miniature Pinschers, you know it goes beyond normal training. There aren't many breeds of dogs out there more stubborn than a Min-Pin, and that stubbornness continues throughout the life of the dog. There is a constant desire to be the alpha-dog and a Min-Pin will push those limits every chance it gets. They are highly intelligent dogs, very trainable. They have minds of their own, however, and whether trained or not, tend to do what they want when they want. As a result, our experience has been that training never stops when you own a Miniature Pinscher.

We have two of this breed in our house, Tazie Woo and Tinker. On average, once a week, we are required to put these two through "reminder sessions" regarding their skills. They are instructed to sit when they do not want to sit. At dinner time, they are instructed to wait for their food when they do not want to wait. These reminder training sessions are required to ensure our girls remember that yes, they are trained and do know commands. (Of course we also do it for the perception that we have at least some semblance of control. No one likes to admit their dog really runs the house!)

When leading a team of people, training is just as important to ensure consistent success of your team. There are 3 types of training...

1) Initial training
2) Refresher training
3) Development training

READY, SET, GO

Initial training sets an employee up for either success or failure depending on the effectiveness of that training. It prepares employees to perform the task for which they were hired. As a manager, it is important that you consistently monitor the effectiveness of initial training ensuring newly hired employees have a positive experience from the get go.

The effectiveness of initial training impacts the new employee's perception of your company and team, impacts the quality of work produced, and ultimately affects employee retention and future turnover. It is also an opportunity for you as the leader to gauge future success.

When an initial training program is run independent of the department, trainers have the tendency to push all new hires out to the floor regardless of their skill sets. Oh, sure, trainers will work with employees who fall behind or new hires that appear to be struggling. There's a point when training has to end and ultimately, the employee is transitioned to the floor.

If you, as the leader, are not involved with the initial training process, that transition makes the employee now your problem. If you are involved, however, you have the opportunity to gauge the employee's skills and make a decision regarding whether or not they should even be given the opportunity to continue.

Hiring and training are costly. If a bad situation is allowed to get worse, re-hiring becomes even more costly. As the leader responsible for the success of your team, get involved in the training process and monitor all your new hires. If you have an independent training program, develop a partnership with that department to ensure success. It is critical that initial training never be taken for granted.

SURE, I REMEMBER THAT

Refresher training acts as a sort of quality control. Employees do not always perform a specific function every day, so refresher training makes sure they maintain their skills even when not using them regularly.

Refresher training is important as a tool to keep teams current on procedures when they are not necessarily located at the same facility. For example, there may be one call center on the East coast and one on the West sharing call volumes. To ensure quality and a seamless experience for customers, all agents need to follow the same procedures. The same principle is at play for production facilities; one plant in Wisconsin and another in Tennessee producing the same product; employees need to follow the same processes to ensure consistent quality for customers.

Refresher training is also a sort of check and balance for the management team regarding changes within the department. Some tenured employees tend to resist change. When new processes are put in place, they will continue with the old way because they think it's better or they may think it's easier. Refresher training involves reviewing things that have changed ensuring people are operating with up to date procedures.

I CAN DO THAT TOO?

Development training is training employees choose to participate in for their own growth. It may be training specific to a new role or promotion they are seeking or training completely unrelated to work. It is something an employee does simply because they want to, and it is something typically of a personal interest. It's also training that can be a great motivator. When presented the opportunity to learn a new skill, it establishes intrinsic value for the team member. When given the opportunity to create and work with you on a personal career development plan, it demonstrates to the employee your recognition of their value and belief that they have potential contributions to be made in the future. This in turn builds the employee's confidence and ultimately their level of engagement with the company.

Imagine you have an employee struggling with productivity. After 9 months of working with the employee s/he is still not meeting the minimum expectation. Most managers think it's time to cut their losses and performance manage the employee out of the organization. A leader, however, will recognize all opportunities before making that decision. Sometimes an employee's issue with productivity has nothing to do with actual productivity.

This is an opportunity to have a conversation regarding real challenges and the source of the employee's struggle. It's also an opportunity to implement a development plan based on that struggle. For some employees self-confidence is the issue. They may be second guessing their work not realizing the impact to productivity. Second guessing is often due to a lack of self-confidence, and if you can build that confidence, the productivity issues are sure to turn around.

Try implementing a development plan that involves having the employee join a committee or volunteer with a non-profit outside of work. Building self-confidence will in and of itself reduce the amount of second guessing because employees believe in themselves.

LEADER AS TRAINER

As the leader, when you take time out of your schedule (and get out of your office) to train a small group of employees, it demonstrates your commitment to the team as well as to those individuals.

Better yet, when you as the leader, take time to sit in on a training session led by an employee, it demonstrates respect for your team as well as an understanding that you don't know everything. You are willing to learn. (A habit hopefully some will emulate.)

And, if you take 15 minutes out of your staff meeting to train your management team on a leadership principle (perhaps one from this book), it demonstrates a commitment to developing leadership skills along with a willingness to share your knowledge.

TRAINING IS PART OF LIFE

Consider such things as the Olympics and professional sports. Training is required in order for athletes to compete in these events. In fact, it's on-going training that becomes routine. My Miniature Pinschers are put through on-going training to ensure they remember their skills. Why shouldn't on-going training be part of your team's development? It can only lead to increased productivity, enhanced quality, and a motivated, engaged team striving to do their best.

Ultimately, dogs want to please their owners, which is why training them is successful. Employees are no different. They want to do a good job and as their leaders, it is your job to set them up for success through training.

Chapter 5

Provide Plenty of Positive Feedback

"Celebrate what you want to see more of."

—Thomas J Peters

The one thing Taz has learned (and taught us) above all else is that positive reinforcement dictates future behavior way more successfully than punishment. Punishing Taz for doing something wrong is really only punishing ourselves. She literally sulks when punished. She slinks off to a corner, puts her sad little face flat on the floor, and stares expressing 100% guilt. Combine that with her floppy little ears and big, brown eyes looking up at us and there is just no way to feel good about what we've done. Somehow, she convinces us that we are actually at fault.

On the flip side, give her a treat for doing something well and it's just the opposite. It only takes approximately two rewards and she remembers whatever it is you're trying to teach her.

We started with rewarding her for going potty outside. My partner would come home from lunch and let the girls outside. When they would come back in, they got a treat. Well, at some point, Taz figured out that if she ran down the steps and ran back up, she could trick us and get a treat without going potty. When we realized what she did, rather than send her back out, we gave her the treat and THEN sent her back out. (She is just so darn cute, how could we not?) Guess what? Taz now gets a treat for going out and another for going potty. I can't wait for the day she trains me to give her a 3rd treat.

We also had an issue with Taz climbing up on the furniture while we were eating. She is a quick, sneaky little bugger and can be quite creative. Thanks to the pins in her knees, she is a somewhat bionic little dog and as a result has figured out how to jump on the back of the couch. She has a very strong, what we call chicken neck, and can pull herself up onto a chair just by using her body for leverage. She figured out how to walk across the table to get at someone sitting on the end of the couch...you name it, regardless of where you are eating, she has figured out a way to get in your lap. From there, it only takes seconds and she has snapped a mouthful of food from your plate. To combat that, we trained her to "wait". She sits attentively waiting while we eat and when finished, she gets a small bite of bread or a piece of carrot; she is rewarded for waiting. That too only took about two tries to train her and now she expects food every time we sit down to eat. EVERY TIME...she even gets a crumb if snacking on a cookie or popping a piece of left over lasagna in my mouth.

When leading people, positive feedback is just as successful. It is important to employee performance, morale, and engagement that each individual feel like they are a contributing member of the team. Timely recognition of positive performance helps reinforce that belief.

INDIVIDUAL ACCOMPLISHMENTS

For individual performance issues, employees need to know that they are not working in vain. As leaders, employees can be motivated through either recognition of individual accomplishments or recognition of team achievements. Individual accomplishments may include productivity improving by 1 item per hour? Maybe the employee arrived on time for work 5 days in a row? Each of these achievements is not significant in and of itself, however, for the individual employee, recognition of the achievement shows several things:

- I can do this. With just a little focus, I was able to improve. With a little more focus, I can do even better.
- My manager cares and recognizes I'm improving.
- I positively affected the team. If I do a little better, the team does a little better and if the team does a little better, we are rewarded.

INDIVIDUAL RECOGNITION IDEAS

Some creative ideas for recognizing individual accomplishments involve pocket praise cards, goofy certificates, most improved awards, traveling trophies, "company bucks" or points that can be accumulated to purchase extra time off, and "You Rock" stones that are passed out when someone does something that "Rocks!" (Get it...rocks for something that rocks?)

TEAM ACCOMPLISHMENTS

Team achievements may include getting an order out before the due date, reaching a monthly or quarterly sales/revenue goal or simply all participating in a charity drive and reaching the fund raising goal.

Recognition of team achievements leads to:

- Increased morale
- Improved team performance
- Team cohesion

Punishment, on the other hand, is de-motivating and leads to discouragement. Employees get frustrated. It decreases self-esteem and can also lead to quality issues. Providing positive feedback acts as a form of intrinsic motivation encouraging both individuals as well as the team.

TEAM RECOGNITION IDEAS

Some ideas of ways to recognize your team are letting everyone go home 15 or 30 minutes early, buying lunch for the team or having pizza brought in for break, or taking a group picture and publishing it with an article about the accomplishment on the company intra-net.

CONSTRUCTIVE FEEDBACK

Part of positive feedback also involves constructive feedback. As a leader, you do yourself and employees no favors if you're not willing to provide honest, constructive feedback. That means being up front regarding the challenges and also including the employee in the solution.

Facilitate a discussion with the employee probing them regarding the problem. Ask them to brainstorm all the possible reasons for their struggles and then ask them to tell you what they need to improve. If the employee asks you for additional training, it will be effective. If the employee asks you for a time study, it will be effective. If the employee asks you for a mentor, it will be effective. If you TELL an employee s/he needs additional training, a time study, or mentoring, it will fail. Include employees in feedback sessions to help drive success.

THE ONE DAY PUSH

Positive feedback can be useful in the promotion of short term achievements. I remember the day before a long holiday weekend and my team was acting squirrelly. Nobody really wanted to be there that day and their minds were off in vacation land. To ensure we maintained our regular level of production for the day, I challenged them with the reward of leaving early. I agreed to let everyone go home 2 hours early if by that time, they could complete the same number of items they would normally complete in an 8 hour period. This meant there needed to be no talking, absolutely no socializing, no extra breaks, and dedicated focus to the task at hand. My Supervisors joined in the challenge by offering to run errands for the employees, so they could continue to work. Need a soda? Need a snack? Need a copy from the printer? Employees called their Supervisor or should I say personal gopher for the day. In the end the team actually completed more than the normal volume from an 8 hour day and they achieved the reward of going home early. I was a hero for the day because they got to go home early and in my eyes, they were heroes for the day because they maintained production. This isn't a technique that works if used on a regular basis, but if utilized effectively, it can lead to great short term accomplishments.

KEEP 'EM GUESSING

One caution regarding positive feedback and tangible rewards...if used consistently, they are no longer rewards but become an expectation.

Taz has received enough treats for going outside that she now thinks she should get one every time. Starting at 8:00 pm every night she walks out to her kennel, comes inside, and sits by her treat jar. After 10 minutes or so, she'll go back outside and repeat the process. This will continue until we eventually go to bed and she gets her final treat for the night.

Likewise, if employees are rewarded with 30 minutes of extra time off every quarter, they will begin to expect this reward whether they meet the objectives or not. The connection between performance and reward is lost and the reward becomes the norm. If you have a habit of buying lunch as a reward for completing an order, after two or three such rewards, employees will expect it and lunch is no longer a reward. Be careful with rewards. Switch them up. Be creative. Present them for various reasons at various times.

Through positive feedback comes great achievement. Be sure to recognize and reward your employee's individual accomplishments as well as team achievements no matter how large or small.

Chapter 6

Let Them Have Fun

"The most wasted of all days is one without laughter."

— E.E. Cummings

When watching Taz attempt to play with her sisters, it needs to be noted that "play" is a personal definition. Taz is 6-lbs of naughty and her idea of playing is really more like tormenting. Our 3rd dog, Erin, was some sort of shepherd mix who loved to play retrieve. (You know it as catch, but after 13 years, Erin was no longer the agile, energetic dog of her youth. She was now the clumsiest, doofiest, most uncoordinated dog, so she rarely if ever actually caught the ball.) Taz also loved to play with the ball; however, her idea of playing was stealing the ball from Erin.

Erin would run across the yard, wait for the ball to hit the ground, pick it up and start running back to the porch only to have Taz jump and snarl at her making her drop the ball. This would go on three or four times as Erin slowly but surely made her way back to the porch. Taz never actually wanted the ball, but she did not want anyone else to have it either. Once Erin got back to the porch, I would bend over to pick up the ball and Taz would steal it one more time only to run three feet away and drop it.

For leaders, letting your employees have fun from time to time is important because it builds a sense of team, engages your group, promotes creativity, drives performance, and reduces turnover. What is important to remember is that "fun" is a personal definition. Just as Taz thought stealing the ball was fun, Erin probably didn't, but I could not begrudge Taz her ideal. Everyone needs to have fun once in a while and they should be entitled to their own kind of fun. Your employees are no different. Their idea of fun may be different than yours, but as long as it is not illegal, causing physical or emotional harm, or creating a liability for the company, let them have fun.

GOOFY GOES A LONG WAY

Try wearing a Safari hat and walk through your department or work area saying to individual employees, "I'm on the hunt for good employees. Have you seen any?"

Does your company conduct a "Jail and Bail" for charity? If yes, come dressed in an inmate costume. Want to make it even more fun? Break out of jail and hide out in different departments. Next thing you know, the whole building will be looking for you and the director will be offering a reward for your capture.

Have a joke of the week, but strive to make it the silliest joke ever. You know, the type told by 2nd graders. I went through my department on March 4 very seriously asking employees if they knew what holiday it was. People guessed all sorts of answers. The final answer was, "March 4 is the only day of the year the calendar tells you to do something. Get it? March Forth." I got plenty of eye rolls over that one, but they laughed.

How about a "Whose Your Daddy" contest? Have employees bring in a picture of their dad and then let everyone guess who belongs to whom.

If in an office environment, try tossing a beach ball over the wall and see if anyone hits it back. If you're lucky, it will keep making it's way around the team.

EVERYONE LIKES A CHALLENGE

Some employees respond to a challenge. A good quarterly reward for great achievement is a ½ day golf outing. Take your top three performers for a half day of golf (or miniature golf for those of you with an uncontrollable slice). How about an afternoon at a major league baseball game? Or an afternoon boat trip? Great accomplishments deserve great rewards. Your employees work hard over the course of a quarter, so if they exceed expectation, let them know it's appreciated.

TEAM BUILDING

The team who plays together stays together. OK, maybe not, but team building certainly helps. Your employees can coordinate monthly or quarterly team building exercises which serves as a development opportunity. It also gets people working together who normally do not interact. Jeopardy games and trivia games related to work are options, or how about a rodeo golf tournament. Place people who normally do not work together on teams and it provides an opportunity for getting to know others on the team.

If you need to teach a sales technique, how about setting up a challenge? You could hand out tickets (representing money) to your employees and then have two agents attempt to "sell" things like cracker jack snacks, licorice twists, peanuts, etc. The agent who sells the most wins. Put a baseball theme to the day, reward a baseball cap for your favorite local team as the prize, and add on a tail gate party for lunch and you've accomplished several things: Motivation, Fun at Work, Development Training, and Positive Feedback.

Some additional ideas for fun in the work place are: A themed food day (Chili cook off, BBQ, Red, White and Blue Food, etc.), Dress down days, Anniversary celebrations, Sponsor a collection for a local charity with team competitions and rewards for the team who collects the most, Happy hour during work hours (with root beer of course).

Life (and work) is nothing if not fun.

Chapter 7

Pay Attention to Detail

"Setting a goal is not the main thing. It is deciding how you will go about achieving it and staying with the plan."

— Tom Landry

For Taz, one of her most favorite things to do (with the exception of anything naughty), is watching. Watching what, you ask? Well, it really does not matter. She watches the neighbors, pays attention to every car that turns around in the driveway, observes kids walking home from school, and at times even watches television. Her heaven is a sunny spot to lie and something to watch. There were times I wish she could talk just to tell me what the neighbors were up to.

Through all of that watching, Taz also never misses a detail. She will bark at a squirrel two lots away, jump instantly to her feet when she hears the neighbors back door just begin to open, will run full speed to the back of the garage when she remembers there are strawberry plants back there, and when she sees the cat walk to another room, she will follow if for no other reason than curiosity. (Our cat has a tendency to knock things onto the floor which at times means an extra treat for the dogs, and Taz NEVER misses an opportunity to get a treat.)

Watching (or paying attention to details) is just as interesting for leaders. In fact, it can be a critical element in determining your success.

FAVORITE VS. MOST RESPECTED

Employees most "favorite" managers tend to be those who do not pay attention to detail. Managers who are laid back, social personalities more concerned with being a friend than a boss. This is a valuable personality in the world of sales; however, it doesn't do much if your group is one of production. Social managers of this nature often find themselves playing catch up. When asked for performance statistics, they need to compile them. When confronted about a disciplinary issue, they need to follow up. When work gets back logged, they are the last to know and scramble to put a plan in place to correct the issue. Complaints of favoritism are also common with these managers. Because their "friends" with employees, other team members resent that friendship resulting in hurt feelings. Some make accusations of favoritism and in some cases those accusations are true. Being a buddy makes being a boss easier, but it doesn't necessarily make it more rewarding.

On the converse, employee's most "respected" managers are those who DO pay attention to detail. Monitoring daily performance holds employees accountable. Observing trends in volumes and performance allows you to be proactive putting plans in place to correct issues before back logs develop. Establishing and reinforcing clear expectations sets the team up for success by avoiding perceptions of favoritism and setting a tone that everyone is treated fairly.

Paying attention to detail also helps establish levels of trust in direct reports, indirect reports, and even your manager.

When direct and indirect reports know you are a manager who pays attention to details, they are more engaged because they know you treat everyone fair. They strive to exceed expectations because they know you will be proud of their achievement. This is an opportunity for them to shine. (Some will even enjoy pointing out a detail you missed.)

Paying attention to details ensures you notice inventory challenges before they become larger issues. It gives you a strong understanding of the everyday challenges impacting your team. It helps regarding utilization of resources creating an environment where you can plan for increases and decreases of work load.

Paying attention to detail puts you in touch with the production side of your business.

CONNECT WITH YOUR TEAM

Paying attention to detail, when managing people, puts you in tune to extrinsic issues that will potentially impact your team. Your employee who rarely smiles walks in smiling...ask them why? Something good happened which they would probably like to share. A dedicated employee with longer than average tenure suddenly cleans off his desk taking home all personal items...why? Is he planning on quitting? He is probably disengaged due to something that happened and as the leader you want to know what it is. Flowers appear on someone's desk...what is the occasion? Everyone is gathered around Sara's desk and you know that she makes the best Peanut Butter Rice Krispy bars...did she by chance bring in a pan today?

Paying attention to detail puts you in touch with the personal side of your business.

MANAGING UP

When your director or manager knows you pay attention to detail, s/he will trust and empower you to do your job. There will be less questioning, less review, and fewer audits; more discussions involving strategy, more projects and challenges sent your way, and more conversations surrounding accomplishments and personal development. When your boss trusts you, it creates a more engaging environment for both. S/he knows you can be counted on to present issues and challenges meaning in turn that s/he does not have to check up on the department. It is a sort of reward for paying attention.

That level of trust can also open doors for you regarding career advancement. One of the secrets to getting ahead is having other people within the organization speaking positively of you.

KNOW WHAT YOU'RE TALKING ABOUT

At one time or another (hopefully not that often), you will be involved in a meeting or sitting on a conference call when your boss agrees to something that's not true. (Unfortunately, some managers are more concerned with their egos than the job at hand.) As a new leader, make sure you know what you're talking about before speaking. If you're unsure, admit it or better yet, ask one of your employees to answer.

I had a boss at one point who during a conference call with compliance told the team that we followed a process in question and had reporting around that process. Problem was, we didn't. Due to her lack of knowledge and love to hear herself talk, there was a lot of back peddling after the call explaining to compliance representatives one on one what our actual processes entailed.

If you pay attention to detail, your team will pay attention to detail and you can hopefully avoid situations like the one above.

LIFE GOES ON DURING VACATION

One additional detail to consider is what happens when you're on vacation. Let's say your company conducts a three week time study regarding computer usage and the deadline to submit your information is during the week you're on vacation. What happens if you fail to submit the data on time? The project team assumes there was no impact to your group and when new computers are ordered, your team gets none. Sound a little far fetched? It isn't. It happened. How would you like to be the one tasked with explaining to the team why everyone in the building is getting new computers with the exception of them?

Business decisions are made every day with strong regard for deadlines. If you miss a deadline, there are a number of repercussions that could result. Miss a budget deadline and lose money (or head count) for the upcoming year. Miss a promotional deadline and your product could be excluded from the upcoming sales catalogue. Miss an HR deadline and you could lose bonus money for your employees.

Part of your responsibility as the leader is ensuring work continues in your absence. In fact, one of the best testaments to your leadership strength is exactly how well your team performs in your absence.

Chapter 8

Think Outside the Box

"If everyone is thinking alike then somebody isn't thinking."

—George S. Patton

Have you ever considered that your food may taste better if eaten upside down? Taz has. When she was a puppy, our bigger dogs would steal her food. To protect her, we would place her dish on the kitchen counter and hold her while eating. Taz would then proceed to walk her hind legs up our chest and stomach leaving her balancing on her front paws while eating her food. We never understood why, but time after time, this is the position she would take to eat. Our only conclusion is the food must have tasted better this way. Taz was thinking outside the box.

Taz has always been naughty as well which is also a result of her thinking outside the box. We had friends over for lunch one afternoon. It was a sunny, warm July day and we were eating outside when Taz decided she wanted to go swimming. Now, swimming in her pool (yes, she had her own pool) would have been normal. Taz decided to go swimming in her water dish instead. She walked across the porch, jumped in her water dish, splashed for a few seconds and then walked back over to the other side of the porch. Why? Who knows? (It provided great entertainment for our guests, however.)

There was also the day Taz decided she wanted to eat some strawberries. Normal thought process would be to eat the strawberry directly from the plant, but not for Taz. She pulled one strawberry from the plant located behind the garage, walked it up to the porch, and repeated this process until she had five berries lined up on the porch. (Lean and Kaizen are not her thing.) She then lied down with the berries between her paws and systematically ate each one. Why? Who knows? The point is Taz has always had her own way of doing things.

FIND NEW AND BETTER WAYS

When leading a group of people, being able to think outside the box can lead to process improvement ideas, great motivational ideas, and unexplainable accomplishments. Outside the box thinking is why old bed frames now make great raised flower beds, canisters make utensil holders, and old wash tubs make fabulous flower planters.

My partner currently works for one of the larger banks in America and when working as the manager of their loss prevention unit, she uncovered an area of fraud impacting the company. Long story short, she implemented a "funds hold" process to address the fraud resulting in loss mitigation for the bank of over $3.5M. That little funds hold process was later brought up at a national banking conference as a best practice within her organization and has since developed into a nationwide procedure that's been adopted by other large banks. It was a local problem with a unique solution developed because of outside the box thinking, and it grew to a national best practice due to additional outside the box thinking.

BE CREATIVE

Some additional examples involve creative scheduling for employees and shared resources.

I had one employee who needed to work fewer hours due to a family conflict, however, she needed to remain full time. We made an agreement that I'd let her work 35 hours, however, she needed to maintain her productivity at her current performance. That commitment made such a difference to her that her productivity actually improved. She was doing more in less time, so it was a win-win for both.

Another idea, when your volumes drop and you have extra resources, you have two choices: 1) Send employees home or 2) cross train them on work for another department and lend your resources. Option 2 develops relationships, provides a development opportunity, and is great networking.

Be open, be willing to consider alternatives, and be creative. You have only greatness to achieve.

Chapter 9

Tenacity

"The only difference between a successful person and others is not a lack of strength, nor a lack of knowledge, but rather a lack of will."

— Vince Lombardi

While working in the kitchen one evening, my partner heard a loud crash and running into the living room found Taz lying on the hard wood floor motionless. It appeared as if she had fallen off the back of the couch. Over the course of the next week, we noticed many changes in Taz's behavior and demeanor.

Taz started pacing around the house. She would just walk with no apparent intention or destination in mind and we noticed she was bumping into things for no apparent reason. At one point, I gave her a treat and she snapped catching my finger in the process. I yelled not understanding why she did this because she has never snapped for a treat. Taz is a dainty little girl and she has always eaten both food and treats like a lady at a tea party. And, on a Saturday afternoon, we noticed while sitting on the floor with her, Taz was turning her hind legs and feet inward.

We believed that the fall off the back of the couch resulted in some kind of brain trauma. An initial consultation with our vet resulted in testing for diabetes and possible hormone issues. Those tests were negative. A 2nd consultation with a different vet resulted in us being told Taz may have a slow brain bleed at the base of her brain and we needed to take her to the University of Wisconsin Veterinarian Hospital for an MRI. At this point, absolute fear set in. Taz is our baby and how could we have let this happen?

Our consultation with the University of Wisconsin Veterinary Hospital did not, however, result in an MRI. The doctor performed a different test on Taz's eyes resulting in a diagnosis of S.A.R.D.S. (Sudden Acute Retinal Deterioration Syndrome). The vet informed us that over the course of the last 2—3 weeks, Taz was loosing her eye sight and was now in fact completely blind.

She fell off the back of the couch because she misjudged that jump due to lack of 100% vision. She snapped at me for a treat because she couldn't see it, but could smell it. She was pacing around the house because she was working through a process of cognitive mapping. She was committing our floor plan to her memory, so she could find her way around. And, turning in her hind legs was due to her lack of confidence. She was in a room that she was unfamiliar with and it was her way of turning inward as protection.

The only way I can describe our reaction was devastation. There was a lot of crying on our part, however, none from Taz. Ironically, Taz adjusted to her blindness better than we did.

Over the course of the next couple of months, we watched Taz establish a routine and adjust to her new environment. She learned to feel for the step in her kennel. She learned to pause at the edge of the couch before jumping up or down. We literally put up bumper pads throughout the house to protect her head and Taz uses them to navigate. She brushes against each wall/pad and moves to the next to determine where she is or what room she is entering.

Her personality changed. She tried to keep jumping and spinning, however, stopped because she lost her balance. She wasn't sure where she was when done spinning. She stopped barking and stopped playing with her toys. And obviously, she stopped watching. Her world was now black.

What has amazed us the most, however, is the tenacity she has displayed. Within the last few weeks, she has again started barking. The sound of her shrill little voice which used to send us looking for ear plugs is now a welcome sound. When she wants a treat or wants up on our lap, she has started crying again. It is her way of telling us she wants something. She now scratches at the door when she wants to go in the back yard, and last week, she climbed her way onto the patio furniture in our screen porch. She has started trying to play with her toys. She hasn't quite mastered that, but she is trying which is the important part. She's started spinning and jumping again at breakfast. This is when Taz is the most confident because she knows exactly where she is, so she's comfortable spinning. And, she has a new way of "watching". She is still lying in the yard, but we see her nose do more sniffing in the air now. She has figured out quite successfully how to exist in her new world.

NEVER LET THEM SEE YOU SWEAT

Consider this scenario: Your company is going through a conversion which involves moving a function from one location to another. It's a 1:1 move meaning you have to hire and train 25 employees within three months. Oh, and did I mention, you are the new leader of the team and do not know the processes. In addition, there are other functions throughout your building going through similar conversions, so you're competing against your peers for candidates to hire.

Accomplishing this feat involves the following:

- Creating a plan regarding hiring, training, volume transfers, and system implementations.
- Partnering with other departments regarding interviewing and hiring. If peers come across a candidate who would be a good fit for your area, they refer them over and vice versa.

- Developing a step training program, so new hires can be trained as they are hired.
- Working as many hours as necessary (PM, Weekend, etc.)
- Reviewing the plan and making adjustments as required

It also involves being the cheerleader of your team, telling them you know the team can accomplish this (even though you think the deadline is too tight), and remaining positive when others are unsure.

Do you think this scenario seems a little far fetched? Well, it's not. I watched it happen. I also watched my manager do whatever it took all with a positive and optimistic approach. She empowered our team by assigning projects. She followed up to make sure we were on track with deadlines. She encouraged us and rewarded us. And, through it all, she even managed to conduct some employee development as well as learn the processes she was about to take on. She exhibited tenacity.

TENACITY IS YOUR STRENGTH

When faced with what seem to be impossible circumstances, your level of tenacity defines who you are as a leader. For Taz, tenacity is what kept her going. She adjusted to her blindness doing whatever was required to get back to the life style to which she had become accustomed. No matter how many times she bumped into a wall or tripped on her kennel step, she continued. She is now to the point that visitors can't tell she's blind. Her life is 90% back to the way it was.

As a leader, you can only hope to have half the tenacity that Taz has displayed, however, you will need whatever you can find. There will be impossible project deadlines, last minute process changes, corporate structure changes, reports that are incomplete, huge fluxes in volumes that were unplanned, machines that go down, servers that fail...need I go on? Through it all, you will be expected to maintain your leadership and that takes tenacity. Whatever the circumstance, realize that there is a team of people relying on you and relying on your leadership. Quickly adjusting to the new environment will be required and will also define part of your strength as a leader. It will ultimately result in gaining the respect of your team which makes it worth all the effort.

Chapter 10

Be An Optimist

"Whether you think you can or you can't, you're right."

— Henry Ford

I started this book with Leadership Principle #1—Be an Optimist and I'm finishing with a repeat of the same principle because of the sheer importance and value associated with that principle.

As I review Taz's life and all of the challenges she has faced combined with all of the accomplishments, her attitude (i.e. optimism) is the one quality that resonates through my mind and through every story. It is the one quality that should also resonate through your own leadership experiences. Attitude IS everything.

Responsibilities will change, senior leadership will come and go, vision/mission of your company will be altered, jobs will be lost, promotions will be achieved, etc. If you maintain an optimistic, positive attitude, it will serve you well.

As the leader, your attitude sets the tone for your team.

As a person, your attitude sets the tone for your life.

Taz is proof that regardless of the circumstance with just 6-lbs of determination, 6-lbs of optimism, and a little personality a lot can be accomplished.

It's the Tazie Effect!

Appendix A

Coaching Tips for Learning Development and Training Managers

For some individuals, being a leader is almost destiny. It is part of who they are and people naturally follow. For others, being a leader is a choice. Maybe they want the title, maybe they want more money. There are various reasons for becoming a leader, but my point is that whether natural born leaders or not, everyone new to a leadership position needs to develop their skills.

As a manager responsible for leadership development within your organization, you can enhance the leadership skills of your potential and new managers through coaching based on principles outlined in this book.

"The Tazie Effect" provides a wonderful outline for training basic leadership skills week by week or month by month. That outline can be related to your specific company or to things like operating principles or corporate values. Each story lends itself to discussion encouraging employees to learn from each other.

Suggestions for using "The Tazie Effect" are as follows:

Provide every new leader a copy of the book—Providing new leaders a base to build on is critical to their success and by providing them "The Tazie Effect" stories and principles, you're demonstrating a commitment to their success. Tell them the principles will be referenced at various points throughout the year in different training sessions, so it's important they familiarize themselves with the principles early on.

Develop monthly coaching or training sessions based on each chapter—Having 10 principles lends itself to a successful, year long training program. Typically, performance reviews are conducted at the start of the calendar year. Once completed, you can train 1 principle per month for the remaining part of the year. At the end of the year, it gives the new leader something to reflect back on before the next review cycle. Why not have monthly meetings with all new leaders or potential leaders and coach to the organization as a whole?

Have one-on-one mentoring sessions with new leaders—These principles can also be utilized as one-on-one mentoring sessions. As a manager, discuss each principle at the start of the month and ask your new leader to report back next month regarding implementing the principle. They give you a good starting point for development discussions.

Use the principles to develop presentation skills—Challenge either a new leader or a tenured leader to present one of the principles to your group identifying how it impacted their team. This gives the individual an opportunity to build and strengthen their presentation skills.

Conduct team building practice sessions—Team building is mentioned throughout the book as a way to have fun, develop skills, and motivate employees. Not everyone, however, is skilled at facilitating a team building session. Have your training group brainstorm ideas for a team building event and then execute it among the group. This provides new leaders a safe, non-threatening environment to practice facilitating a team building session before leading such an event for their own team.

Brainstorming sessions—Each of the principles make a great jumping off point for brainstorming. Ask your new leaders to come up with ideas for ways to put people first, have fun at work, provide feedback, or implement development training.

Part of learning is sharing, and discussing these principles, creates a great environment for employees to share ideas, best practices, and other suggestions.

Ask your leaders...Did you have the Tazie effect today?

Bibliography

Quotations listed throughout the book are from one of the following book or internet sources:

Karvelas, K. (1988). *The Essence of Attitude*. New Jersey: Career Press.

Karvelas, K. (1988). *The Best of Success*. New Jersey: Career Press.

Karvelas, K. (1988). *Commitment to Excellence*. New Jersey: Career Press.

Karvelas, K. (1988). *Winning with Teamwork*. New Jersey: Career Press.

Karvelas, K. (1988). *The Magic of Motivation*. New Jersey: Career Press.

www.quotationspage.com

The Tazie Effect

QUICK ORDER FORM

E-mail orders: Orders@pentechprofessional.com

Postal orders: Pen-Tech Professional Services
PO Box 7123
Appleton, WI 54912

Phone orders: 1-920-982-5697

Please send the following # of copies:

_____ x $12.95 = _______

5.5% Sales Tax = _______

(sales tax required only if a State of WI resident)

Shipping = _______

($4.00 for 1st book/$2.00 for each additional copy)

Total Enclosed: _______

Name: ________________________________

Address: ________________________________

City: ________________________________

State: __________ **Zip:** ____________________

Telephone: ______________________________

E-mail: ________________________________

The Tazie Effect

QUICK ORDER FORM

E-mail orders: Orders@pentechprofessional.com

Postal orders: Pen-Tech Professional Services
PO Box 7123
Appleton, WI 54912

Phone orders: 1-920-982-5697

Please send the following # of copies:

______ x $12.95 = ________

5.5% Sales Tax = ________

(sales tax required only if a State of WI resident)

Shipping = ________

($4.00 for 1st book/$2.00 for each additional copy)

Total Enclosed: ________

Name: ______________________________

Address: ______________________________

City: ______________________________

State: __________ **Zip:** ______________

Telephone: ______________________________

E-mail: ______________________________